This anthology shows just how poetry can matter—for a community, from a community and by a community. Holmes, Weiss, and Weems describe the synergy between artist and populace as they give their perspectives from "the greenest, leafiest streets" of the Heights to "the real picture, the cold gray one...where winter has us by the icicles," from the bustle of Coventry to the lawns of Oakwood, from the Lee Road Library to Cain Park, they have their ears to the streets and pens to the pulse of this diverse neighborhood that is a microcosm of Cleveland.

—Ray McNiece, author of *Our Way of Life*

Bottom Dog Press
and
HEIGHTSARTS

Awake at the End:
A Heights Arts Poet Laureate Anthology

Meredith Holmes
Loren Weiss
and
Mary E. Weems

Edited by
John Panza and Mary E. Weems

Bottom Dog Press
Huron, OH

A collaborative production of
Heights Arts & Bottom Dog Press

Bottom Dog Press
PO Box 425/ Huron, OH 44839
http://members.aol.com/Lsmithdog/bottomdog
Heights Arts
2163 Lee Road #104 / Cleveland Heights, OH 44118
www.heightsarts.org

Thanks to the Heights Arts Board of Trustees, the HeightsWrites Committee, Peggy Spaeth, Larry Smith and Bottom Dog Press, Herb Ascherman, JoAnn Dickey, Timothy Callaghan, and the residents of Cleveland Heights, Ohio, for their continued support for the arts.
Of course, we thank our Poet Laureates for generously sharing their work with us here and elsewhere.

CREDITS

Cover Art: Timothy Callaghan
Cover design: JoAnn Dickey
Author Photographs: Herb Ascherman
Layout Design: Susanna Sharp-Schwacke & Larry Smith

ACKNOWLEDGMENTS

Some poems in this book have appeared in various forms in the following publications: *Shubad's Crown, Cleveland in Poetry and Prose, Cleveland Poetry Scenes: A Panorama and Anthology, Good Times for Hard Times, Ohioana, Ohio Writer, Tributaries, Palo Alto Review, I'd Rather Be Flying, An Unmistakable Shade of Red & The Obama Chronicles.*

DEDICATION

For Richard Wallace Clancey—Scholar, Educator, Cleveland Heights Native

—John

For Katie D., Bree, Ben G., Brian T., and all the independent poets

—Mary

CONTENTS

MARY WEEMS, 2007 & 2008 POET LAUREATE

Poems

THE CLEVELAND HEIGHTS POET LAUREATE PROJECT
John Panza

My involvement with the Cleveland Heights Poet Laureate Project began in 2005 with an e-mail from Elisa Meadows, at the time the gallery director at Heights Arts and to this day a friend of mine. A member had dropped off the newly formed Poet Laureate committee—soon renamed HeightsWrites—and this vacancy needed to be filled with an enthusiastic, poetry friendly body. Two pedestrian bullet points on my CV led Elisa to suggest I join the committee: I teach poetry at a local college and I live in Cleveland Heights, enough to convince Peggy Spaeth—Heights Arts' indefatigable director—that I could contribute something to this grassroots project. This Poet Laureate Project, coupled with a rather raucous Heights Arts benefit that I attended with my wife and friends, solidified my involvement with Heights Arts. The three years I have been involved with Heights Arts as a HeightsWrites Committee member, next as a Board Member, and now the host of a Heights Arts radio show, have been fun and rewarding personally and professionally.

Cleveland Heights is a city where an idea for something "community" and "artsy" mentioned in passing to a city council member, the mayor, reporter, business owner, or citizen sitting in Phoenix Coffee can take root and become "something" overnight. That's a really clumsy way of pointing out the ingenuity and genuine community spirit that inhabits Cleveland Heights. That's how Heights Arts got going...and the forces within that organization did the same with the Poet Laureate Project. And nowhere is this notion of Genesis to Revelation in 24 Hours Flat exemplified than in the process—if it can be called a process—that led to the Poet Laureate Project. Like so many of the great ideas in Cleveland Heights, a chance encounter with art resulted in a conversation between residents...and then something happening.

Once a year, the Cleveland Heights-University Heights Public Library closes for a kind of holiday, a library staff professional day. In 2004, Peggy Spaeth was invited to speak to the library staff about Heights Arts. She was given ten minutes. With only a wee bit of coffee and way more than ten minutes-worth of material to share, Peggy was feeling "more than the usual early morning grumpiness" when the day's organizer welcomed the day's participants to the day's activities. The organizer then introduced Ben Gulyas, one of the library staff members and a poet. Ben had composed an occasional poem called "An Invocation for Staff Day 2004," and it proved an epiphany for Peggy and others:

9

An Invocation for Staff Day 2004   by Ben Gulyas

Here we are—a Friday morning in October—
here we are, hoped up, strapped in,
wading through a fog of "what happened to sleep?"
our crumpled socks, our hard toast, our bath water overcrowded
      with ducks...
here we are spiraling in eternity,
a pin prick of Democracy,
peach cobbler & herring bone...
a dreamer's mind envisioned in libraries,
pulled from sleep
to "wake up" "wake up!"
the bee keeper's daughter
rasping a morning's call
to welcome out the barn
the lamb, the goat, the mule,
the cow, the horse,
the crow...
walking Spanish under light poles, down the sun, under the rain...
pulled from sleep into an equinox of coffee and tired shoes—
Here we are staggered and determined,
sweet Mrs. Cline, who lived forever
with all the world,
holding a book in the hand,
wood smoke and cookies
—plotting invocations to the Great Collector, the library
of our treasures—like the spike of the heart
in uncharted waters,
and with a blink of the eye, into the morning
Ahab and Jonah,
stroll from the bar(n)
return to pay their overdues
and criss-cross a few phone numbers for hens' teeth...
and it all
makes sense—

miles to the point
years to right now
one earshot
to the fox—
"Aha!!
Don't throw us in the briar patch!
Don't throw us in the briar patch!"

We are in it now—a Friday morning in October—
so let us begin.

    By the end of Ben's reading, Peggy had "been to places in my own psyche that surprised me," an overwhelming sense of something "beginning." That poem planted a seed that germinated into the Poet Laureate Project, an official, sanctioned Poet Laureate position in Cleveland Heights.

The event reinforced precisely what Heights Arts is all about, elevating local arts for acceptance by a broader audience. Peggy went on to tell others about how nice it would be to have civic events open with poems from local poets, perhaps even a Poet Laureate.

At some point in the day, Peggy's idea got back to Ben, who passed it along to a reporter from the *Plain Dealer* who that evening wandered into Mac's Backs, the locally owned bookstore where Ben also worked. The reporter called Peggy for a comment.

Forty-eight hours after that poem was read aloud to the library staff, there was a front-page metro-section story in the *Plain Dealer* about a Cleveland Heights Poet Laureate, with a quote from the Cleveland Heights mayor Ed Kelley supporting the idea. Yes, a mere forty-eight hours from idea to full civic support. Considering this story, I am reminded of Meredith Holmes' poem "Cleveland Heights Field Notes," which ends with the line: "Only in Cleveland Heights."

In 2005, the HeightsWrites committee convened and began recommending poets for appointment by the City Council. The 2005 Poet Laureate was Meredith Holmes. In 2006, Loren Weiss was appointed. In 2007, Mary Weems was appointed and subsequently recommended for a second term.

And what do Poet Laureates do? To answer that, it is worthwhile to focus on what they don't do. Like everyday poets, Poet Laureates don't do this for the money. The US Poet Laureate gets a stipend of a little more than $35,000/year. The Cleveland Heights' Poet Laureate gets around 1/35th of that. Even though officially appointed by politicians, Poet Laureates are neither politicians nor patsies. They can certainly be political, but never patsies. The Poet Laureate operates outside of the everyday politics of those who appoint them and those they "serve." To paraphrase Auden, the poems make nothing happen. Neither do Poet Laureates. They create private art for public consumption while simultaneously creating public art for private consumption. Independence from political machinations is necessary. Poet Laureates produce occasional poems that ideally inspire citizens and politicians alike to recognize that civic, political, and artistic motives can share a stage.

Cleveland Heights' Poet Laureates read poems at the openings of civic events. They share poems with school kids. They get interviewed by local media. They promote the value of poetry. Their poems are not by nature political, socially relevant, or even often related to the occasion at which they are read. They are merely poems. To quote Archibald MacLeish, "A poem should not mean, / but be." And this objective stance, I would argue, is what awakens in others their subjective creativity.

To this day, there is no Poet Laureate of Cleveland, and even the title of Poet Laureate of Cuyahoga County bestowed upon the late Daniel Thompson was honorary only, unofficial, unsanctioned—not that anything "official" or "sanctioned" made much of a difference to Thompson. The fact is that in a culture where more folks write so-so poetry than read so-good poetry, the bestowing of a Poet Laureate title on a poet, be it official, unofficial, even peer assigned, is not something to be taken lightly. Regardless of the size of the city, county, state, or country, the title Poet Laureate carries with it broad implications. One hears Poet Laureate and thinks of the pantheon of British and American poets, alive and dead. To be given Poet Laureate status is to merge the private and public personas of the poet. The poet is often a solitary creature. But recognize that the public nature of a Poet Laureate position often moves that poet into a public venue that can be somewhat less forgiving than the limited sphere of family, friends, and fellow writers. The poet's move to a fully public persona is unnatural for many. To take that leap is an act of bravery.

You might be thinking, a Cleveland Heights poet elevated to the status of a Wordsworth? Well, no. Wordsworth is Wordsworth. Billy Collins is Billy Collins. But the creation of this Cleveland Heights Poet Laureate Project was not a local thing. A well-respected national newspaper picked up the *Plain Dealer* story of the Cleveland Heights Poet Laureate Project and ran it as part of a story on the resurgence of poetry in the United States.

One last point. In case you don't know much about Poet Laureates, note that *declining* a Poet Laureate offer is an old tradition, something rebellious, like turning down that major label record deal to continue "keeping it real," schlepping your own gear, and eating Ramen noodles in a van. We have been lucky enough not to have anyone deny us, yet. Perhaps because the process in the first few years was application-based we have been blessed with dedicated, affable, well-selected poets. The poets who have embraced this opportunity thus far—Meredith Holmes, Loren Weiss, and my co-editor Mary Weems—took the leap of faith that is the Cleveland Heights Poet Laureate Project as a way of giving back to the community that has in so many ways given much to them: like good restaurants, walkable streets, a solid housing stock, true diversity, above average schools, a nuclear free zone, and an excellent recycling program. Oh, and a fully recognized Poet Laureate position.

As Ted Kooser, a former US Poet Laureate, argues, poetry is a two-way street, a conversation. There is not just the poet. There is not just the audience. There is a poet *and* an audience. Communion is the point. Such communion is seen pointedly in the Cleveland Heights Poet Laureate Project. It is my hope that you will discover your own sense of communion with some of the poems in this book.

Opening the Lines of Communication
Mary E. Weems

Art hurts. Art urges voyages—and it is easier to stay at home.
—Gwendolyn Brooks

Working on this anthology with John has been a pleasure, as has the time I've spent with the work of my fellow Poet Laureates Meredith and Loren.

While I agree with John that many of the poems created by Cleveland Heights Laureates "are not by nature political, [or] socially relevant," writing poems that respond to current and/or past political or social issues is important to me. Like the late artist Gordon Parks my choice of weapon is art, and while I do on occasion write poems that are not of this ilk, I follow a long line of African American poets and others who have used their poems as political acts to speak out against injustice. This is not to say that political, socially relevant poems are better or more poetic than their counterparts; I get something special out of every good poem I read.

I find the common ground of being a woman in Meredith's work. My late grandmother was my best friend and when I read an excerpt from Meredith's poem: "I ran outside and the rain/ was falling so fast, the lane/ was already a river, grabbing pieces/ of pasture and shooting them downhill," I imagine my granny as a young girl, free to roam and play in a sudden downpour. The two of us attended a Lou Suarez workshop at Heights Arts. Later, in another work in this collection Meredith begins a poem with a line by Gerald Stern, "The weeds give up suddenly, after a small struggle." We both attended his poetry workshop at Heights Arts and I end a poem with this same line. Meredith has an unforgettable way of describing the everyday "[p]assing cars spotlight dead weeds/ caught in the chain link fence/and now, falling past/ these rooms of light is snow," and I know I'll turn back to her poems in this anthology again and again to delve deeper into their meanings.

From Loren's poems I get the sweet, poignant lines of distant and not-so-distant memory. He brings the symphony at Severance Hall to life "[g]lorious music flows,/ ebbs, engulfs me/ in rich sonorous waves," and "[p]eriods of unexplained silence/ fester between measures." He reminds me of love happening often unnoticed in nature gracing a backyard "[h]ey Mr. Cottontail,/ I know what you're doing/ you lucky bastard. Why not/ try to kiss her first," of long-time-ago love "[f]inally/ time to tell her/ how I loved her silently,/ in grades seven,/ eight, and nine." Loren leaves me thinking deeply about what it means to be mortal "[w]e drift into our own thoughts,/ not caring to intrude/ on each other's hazy episode./ Look up at clear bag of fluid/ hooked on arms of/ stainless stick-man/ towering above me."

His work has a quiet, poetic way of moving into my spirit for a while, of communicating what it means to be fully alive, open to the ways of a world rushing on to a future only our poems will live to see.

More than anything I want my tenure as Poet Laureate to be remembered as one of using poetry to build a stronger sense of community across race, ethnicity, gender, sexual orientation, class, culture and mental and physical ability. The following poem created using selected slips of paper written by Cleveland Heights children, teens, young adults and adults as part of the Heights Arts "This is Where" map project gives a sense of the many voices that make up a community I've grown to love:

OPENING THE LINES OF COMMUNICATION

This is where...**we do art**, I learned from family how to be funny, I trusted her, I finally found peace, I practice serenity, We buy our favorite bagels, We dance, I feel my mother, She said *yes!* The undead rat was born, I got sober at Club 24, I found a kitten—meow! You smoke, I breathe freely with the water, The sound of Danny's flute used to catch my soul like flypaper, I make history, People gathered to talk about the future, Got the jungle where I feel safe, My father's name is listed as a person who served in WWII, My life ended, A sound of violin is heard, I avoid to go, My high friend broke into an apartment for cash—and found a dead guy, We stood to hold signs, My cats take care of me, Love lives, My heart was, My aunt and uncle worked to keep CH an integrated community, I partied like a rock star at the Slaughter house, I deliver Meals-on-Wheels, I was struck by *lighting* across the street from my house, I make a new beginning and look into the beauty of NOW! I picked my daughter up from school and tried to explain 9-11, I have my lair, I eat ice cream, I first felt at home, I fell flat on my belly in the middle of the road—like Buster Keaton in the middle of traffic, I climbed a tree and got stuck, I grew up a screw up, I sing out loud in my car, There is a maple tree that reminds me of sherbet, We swoop across the floor, I try not to see, Cain Park lives and breathes in a city in need of more trees & fewer cars, This *iz* where I shot 8 dices, and rolled 1,988 7's, I cry at movies, I feel lonely, I go to watch the sunset over the lake, I used to live in my favorite house with a pig stone wall around it, My grandmother attended

14

my sister's wedding wearing a fur stole but no teeth, I became a Joy Spreader, I get inspired, Where we go for comfort & security, Officer West was killed, I first experienced freedom, I STOP! and love myself—no more abuse, I had too much Grey Goose! yumme, I look out my window as I re-create my life, My father shot himself to death, My dog waits, I had a mushroom that grew in my bathtub, The street curves and the houses are large with sloping yards, The first kiss I care to remember, My children made friends with each book they read, We saw the double rainbow, We shooted roots, We buried our pet, I learned my mother died, 3 black cats played, We played drums and sang songs at the lower Shaker Lake, I got arrested, I hear music, I go when I need to cry, Many of my neighbors have become friends, I planted the Jubilee Garden, My little sister was born, I saw a UFO in the summer of 1975 at Shaker Lake, We made a time capsule when renovating a room: glass jar—pix of house and family—letter from me, I wrote a poem, I stop by my favorite little wooden door, The hottest guy I ever dated lived, We made out after our first date in 1976, My son and two cats laugh and live, I was so happy hanging my clothes on the clothesline, I grew up and learned that their addictions didn't have to be mine, My childhood memories exist, I live and dream, I raise[d] my son on my own, I got punched in the nose in the second grade, I lived from 8 to 18—Now I'm 50 but whenever I drive by—I think: who's upstairs in my room— the light's on, I live under the canopy—I nursed my daughter, The nightmare ended, kids are hanging out and are in gangs, I feel overwhelmed held in the world, He called out her name, My car stopped, Healing and wholeness occurred, I got both pizza and a ticket at 3 a.m., My education started—kids are wonderful teachers, She first lived, I taught persons who are blind to cross traffic light intersections for 32 years, I got my first kiss, My grandma lives—My dad grew up—My uncle's ashes were spread—My brother got attacked by poodles—We always ate Jello—and had fake money, The nightmare started, Our hearts became one, An old lady fell down, I saw the Wizard of Oz, **I feel imaginative...**

The poems, which follow represent work created during our individual journeys as Poet Laureate. Each of us still poets, Cleveland Heights residents, and awake at the end.

MEREDITH HOLMES
2005 CLEVELAND HEIGHTS POET LAUREATE

Meredith Holmes grew up in a small Quaker town in New Jersey and started writing poetry in high school. She graduated from Case Western Reserve with a B.A. in English and worked in a variety of writing and editing jobs in Cleveland. Meredith was part of Big Mama, a poetry theater group that performed in Ohio and New York and published two collections of poetry. She is currently part of Take Nine, a group of nine women poets who just staged their first reading.

Meredith's publications include a collection called *Shubad's Crown* (Pond Road Press 2003) and her poems have appeared in Garrison Keillor's *Good Poems for Bad Times* (Viking 2005), *Cleveland in Prose and Poetry* (League Books 2005), and *Cleveland Poetry Scenes: A Panorama & Anthology* (Bottom Dog Press 2008).

THINK, WRITE, LISTEN
Meredith Holmes

When I became Poet Laureate of Cleveland Heights, my relationship to the people of Cleveland Heights—all 50,750 of them—changed. I was no longer an observer—the role I feel most at home in. I had been singled out to speak for, about, and to the people of Cleveland Heights. How to do this? I am no Nikki Giovanni or Nabeel Yasin. I am no Daniel Thompson. I tried to write as honestly as I could about my own experiences and hoped that anyone listening to or reading my poems would be both curious to hear a different point of view and gratified if it spoke to their condition.

I had a big constituency: my daughter, her teachers, her friends, and their parents. The enterprising 10-year-old down the street who started a dog-walking business and my neighbor who has worked in the kitchen at Nighttown for 30 years. All the beauticians, baristas, and bank tellers in town. The unsung city sanitation workers and the stand-up comics at Seitz-Agin hardware. The Emerita professor who owns Appletree Books, the party animals across the street, and the cops who put an end to their festivities. The librarians who do their job, no matter what, and everyone who's ever eaten at Tommy's. My responsibility to the public could have been pen-paralyzing, but it was inspiring to have a live audience—one I could see, hear, and talk to.

As Poet Laureate, I never stopped trying to understand the nature of my mission to bring poetry to public life in Cleveland Heights, and I never stopped trying to answer the question a Cleveland Heights high school student asked: "How will people who are different from you relate to your poems?" Of course everyone is different from me; everyone has their own story. But there are also things that bind us together. To discover these things, a writer must be honest, and she must listen. Being Poet Laureate made me a better listener and a better writer.

SAULTE SAINTE MARIE

Saulte Saint Marie
deserted by the small
fur-bearing mammals
powerless to prevent the retreat
of the sound-swallowing
coniferous forests
waits like a quiet, large-limbed girl
barefoot on the banks
of the St. Mary's river
looking down at the wildflowers
wilting in her big, red hand.

YES, THIS WAS THE RIVER THAT BURNED

"Cuyahoga" means crooked,
but to us it has come to mean
burning river.
The water itself seemed to burn
that June day in 1969.
Reports tell us that flammable toxics:
toluene, benzene, Xylene
and the familiar gasoline
glazing the surface of the Cuyahoga
are really what burned.
But to us, the river, given up
for dead, burst into flame
and fire walked on water, raising
a thunderhead of black smoke,
sought the river bend, and feasted
there on chemical-soaked debris.
There are few pictures
but what image is more memorable
than knowledge held in the body?
This twisting, this perversion
of the possible is part of us now.
"Cuyahoga" means crooked,
but to us it has come to mean
burning river.

CLEVELAND HEIGHTS FIELD NOTES

You'd be surprised at the wildlife here:
I saw a red-tailed hawk
pluck a rock dove from the facade
of Heights Medical Arts
and fly up Fairmount with it.

During the blackout
of course people came outside
lit candles and talked on porches.
All up and down my street we could hear
the usually drowned music of conversation
and in one house—singing.

The rink is frantic on Sunday afternoon
with girls in long skirts
and hockey skates assaulting the turns,
masters of the cross-over and the sudden,
ice-showering stop.

Barbara and I are sitting on the curb
in front of Tommy's.
It's mid-summer, and two beat cops
chug down Coventry
parting waves of revelers
staying the course to Hampshire and back.

Barbara has toured and approved my new place.
"You always pick the greenest, leafiest streets,"
she says, "You'll enjoy the rain there."
I'm suddenly afraid this will be
our last, long conversation.
But it isn't. A year later
we stand in front of Barbara's house
admiring the mail carrier:
his leather bag, his knee socks
and the long, grey ponytail
snaking down his back.
"Only in Cleveland Heights,"
Barbara says.

THE REPUBLIC OF SUMMER

In elevators and take-out lines
we cling to our habit of complaining:
the heat, the humidity
the streets oozing with tar.
Just a month ago it was the cold
the bullying by snow
and the cowardice of spring.
We're swimming in summer
awash in thunder and cicadas
and the distant music of lawnmowers.
But it's all fake, all spin!
We've been cut out and pasted
onto a photograph of summer.
The crisp midday shadows,
the pink, dinner-plate hibiscus—
we fall for it every year
and every year our hearts are broken.
It's no good—put us back
into the real picture, the cold,
gray one, where winter is absolute,
where we have no say
but only endure.

when three boys
two tall and antelope-lanky
and one little, enter the cross-walk.
The tallest rests his palm
flat on the head of the little one
and in his other hand
lightly balances a football.
No lingering at the heartbreak
end of summer for these three.
It's noon, and their shadows
bob along behind them
like small excited dogs.
They wear baggy shorts
and white t-shirts that billow
and ripple in the breeze.
Their legs are too skinny
for this world, but inside them
is all sprinting, all jump shots
all stairs taken two at a time.
They pass in front of my car
deep in conversation,
the little one, trotting beside
hopeful and wary, studying
first their faces, then
the ground they walk on.
They trust I will stay put
and they do not question
that they belong here—
in this moment, in this city
where they move so easily
like boats in a harbor—
lightweight, straight-masted
not quite ready for the open ocean.

First-hand Experience

This happened a long time ago:
A new poet had been discovered.
He would read his prizefighter poem
just once at the Coventry Library
before leaving town for good.
I can't recall the prizefighter
But the poem about his mother
so erect in her overcoat, so angry
the fine white people's dentist
refused to treat her children, who were
just glad she wasn't angry at *them*.
I remember thinking:
My mother seemed taller than she was
and we were more afraid
of her than thunder or God.
And the poem about his father:
How one summer night, everyone
was talking on the porch
but he stood a little apart
out in the yard, looking up
at the stars, shining unfettered
in the soft black sky.
I thought:
So that's how it was with his father.

LIBRARY DOS AND DON'TS

You may not bring a trained
attack dog, even on a leash
to the library.
You may not lie about a lost book
("See, what happened, was...")
Never interrupt a librarian
who is telling you how
to find something, even
if you think she's telling you
way more than you need to know.
And especially if you only asked
a question to distract the librarian
from what she was doing—
i.e., getting ready to throw you out.
If you are engaged in serious research
you may eat a pastrami on rye
in the stacks, but you must be discreet.
Over the years, many poets, novelists
and local historians have survived
this way, eating just a bite
or two at a time.
You may ask for a new card
if yours is tattered and grubby.
There is no shame in this.
As long as you don't have a cold
or the flu, feel free to plunge
your face into a book and breathe deeply
its newness or age and the delight
of the last reader, which lingers
like the smell of vanilla
or wind with rain and thunder in it.
You may not, under any circumstances
play tag in the library.
Although, if the moment is right
and you are standing quite close
in the fiction stacks.
With someone you know
and you're both reading Rumi
or Lorca, but thinking one thought
and *know* you are, then
you may kiss this person.

25

If, however, you plan on doing
more than that, you must both
check out all materials
and leave the library at once.

we will learn to paint.
It will take years to learn
clouds, milk, and skin.
In the studio, you will capture
with conté crayon,
skinny old men in codpieces
ample, gazing women.
And the mysteries of folded cloth.
You will learn perspective,
a trick that disappears
telephone poles and entire
herds of buffalo.
Then we go outside!
In the plein air, you must forget
and remember all
as you paint children
chasing their tails,
the bridge, and the mound
of blankets sleeping under it.
You will bathe trees in both
morning and evening light.
All these things, you will discover,
live their own lives,
separate and unreachable.

You'll love dance!
It's all about you!
Alone, bare feet pointing
east, stuffed into a freight elevator,
You caught like a kite in a tree,
or swinging like a bell
down the street.
Your body teaching you how to listen.
Arm by hip, by heel, your body
becomes fluent in a thousand languages—
some thought to be lost or dead:
birds in the ivy, a struck match,
clean rags ripped
lengthwise for bandages.
Your body will translate everything.

Finally, we will learn to write.
In this class, you will never stop reading.
You'll be lying on the floor
in the living room in summer
and you are bored—maybe
thinking about a root beer float—
and you pull a book from the shelf.
It's *The Last Flower* by James Thurber.
You gulp it down, and the next one,
then *The Screwtape Letters*,
some 1945 *Life* magazines and *Green Mansions*.
Soon you've devoured the whole stack
and you're still hungry.

Certain things will be painful
until you apply the cool
compress of words:
the smooth caves of coffee cups
hanging over the sink,
sudden rain, and the way
your sister stands, ankles kissing
to peer into the refrigerator.
When you get the knack of sitting
down and writing every day
your characters show up
at the front door with a lot of luggage.
They push past and take over the house.
One night, very late
you come downstairs and they're all
sitting at the kitchen table, drinking Pernod,
reading Dashiell Hammett aloud (and laughing).
You stand there in your pajamas
feeling awkward, until one
stands up, scraping back the chair
and asks you to dance.

DRUNKEN SLEEP

I must have dozed off
bathed in the blue light
of the table lamp
when a hungry rat
upset the tea saucer
his tiny bald feet skidding
across my clean ink stone
not rousing me, but twisting
my lovely smooth dream
downward into a ragged
worry of gnawed books
and ravaged pages.
Silly boy, doesn't he know
simple catcalls were never enough
to stop this kind of thing?

SUPER NOVA

I miss you.
I pull up to the light
and hope the beat-up Volvo
is yours, knowing it can't be
because you are so
out of town, light years
away, and the probability
that we will collide
is about a trillion squared to one.

I knew you wouldn't stay.
We don't get many like you
and I can spot a "guest star,"
(as the Chinese call them)
from miles away.

It was shocking—the way you outshone
your parents, your friends, even
your daughter who had such
a steady, pleasant light.
And that tremendous release
of energy in your last moments here—
it mesmerized us, caused us to spin
faster in our orbits, to buy exotic plants
and outrageously expensive picture frames.

All this happened, and then
you escaped the crushing force of gravity
by exploding through your own skin.
This produced a brief intense light
and scattered fertile star debris everywhere.

SARAH

Born the same year
we are each other.
But even at 25
we were as different
as apples and roses.
My skin was toughening
And you still bruised so easily!
Your course was quixotic
and inventive: teaching
children how to sing like whales
and find each other in the tall grass.
Once you took an office job
and lasted exactly one day.
You said moving papers
around was soothing at first
then just meaningless.
I put on pantyhose and
went downtown to work.
I floated on a river
of meaninglessness, building up
a tolerance for ugly commutes
and stale conversation.

You came to potlucks
with a whole pineapple
or a chipped cup
full of blackberries.
We all had the same Gestalt
therapist then, and the same
Zen plumber, who looked great
in blue jeans and black t-shirt.
We speculated endlessly about him.
You were only half there
in this ordinariness, already
beginning to drift away
like a Skellig who thinks only
of returning to the sea.

You showed me Tai Chi
you'd just learned: "Embrace
Tiger, Return to Mountain,"
your long arms and legs describing
vistas of mind and heart
I'd never considered
known were big enough to live in.

Then you leapt into the cold green
water, with its deep, booming chords
each stroke taking you so far, so fast,
and I stood on the hard,
pebbly beach, waving, waving.

The watch has wound down,
its slender golden fingers
finally still, waiting
for us to set the time
to begin again.
We have invited and polished
set cookies on gaudy plates.
We greeted and enjoyed
but now—as we knew they must—
friends file out the door
buttoning their coats
and declaring their intentions
for the coming season:
take long walks, work in the garden
and see more of each other.
April has won the day
chasing us toward forsythia,
mud, and heartbreak.
But we'll step eagerly
into our seats at the bottom
of the Ferris wheel
and rising clockwise
in our gently swaying cups
at the park spinning below:
the opulent greenery
children's white shoes flashing
kites and balloons wriggling free
and the lake—lapping the rim
of its shallow blue bowl
seeing it all again
as if for the very first time.

"WE PAY SO DEARLY FOR OUR JOY"
Bonnie Jacobson

A stocky young woman
jumps the sidewalk puddles
and leaves a vapor trail of sadness
visible even against this
transparent, rain-scrubbed
April morning.

Lists, especially the ones you find
in the pocket of a winter coat
on the first cold day, are sad.
You are putting on the new season
reaching into pockets
for something familiar
and find the reason
for writing things down
has passed.

Graduations are sad—
the solemnity and the gaiety.
Lanky children striding ahead
Graying parents lingering
in the shadow of the bell tower

Garage sales and the flocks
of buyers gazing at bowls
and boxes of big
dusty shoes are sad.
But so is the way the sellers
baring their souls
on tables set in the driveway
can't look you in the eye.

The poet, mouth agape
sleeping all day
in her angled hospital bed
waking at sundown and asking
Am I alive? Am I Rose?

From My Grandmother's Diary

"Flag Day! Very sultry.
Pop finished haying in the forenoon.
Drank lemonade on the porch.
Ants on the peonies.
Played canasta after supper
and finished the elderberry pie.
Wind kicked up about 8.
Thunderheads over the barn
looked like mountains
finally coming to us!
I ran outside, and the rain
was falling so fast, the lane
was already a river, grabbing pieces
of pasture and shooting them downhill
orange daylilies still on.
Just before dark, Ruby's horse
got loose and ran right up to me
no bridle, and all shining wet.
She let me jump on and we took
off east on the Star route.
I don't remember much
after that, just felt like we
were running into a wall
of noise and dark, sometimes
over hard road, sometimes soft grass
and by morning, I was set down
in a whole new clean place."

Lizzie just about lived at my house.
We ran barefoot all over town
proud of our calluses
our flying-dismount bike skills
our big-brother-evading finesse.
We played hearts and war
checked our vaccination scars
forded creeks and spied on nuns.
But this whole time, Lizzie never knew
I communed with trees
knew the furred undersides of leaves
and how they cupped rain.
I read the day, felt its forehead
for fevers, watched
from the doorway If it was restless
walked away when it slept peacefully.
I was alert to the cross-talk of jays
and hand-mowers, the constant
musical confetti of songbirds.
A bike thrown down in the wet grass
Wasps with their feet caught in the screen.
The tone and timbre of everything
how it all hung together
like a great wide weaving
open to the wind and strung with bells
and how I was knotted into it
so that running and singing
were always the same thing.

say, "East River" and "Adlai Stevenson"
and the summer sportscasters chanting
"high and outside," hypnotizing us all.
I miss rocketing past the NJ turnpike
sign that said *New York and North*
and I miss my grandmother
saying, "hark!" and the way
she smelled, like hay and mint
and how she sat on her leg
reading, and the way my mother
nagged her, "stop that, you know
it makes you bow-legged!"
But my mother did it, too,
reading late at night in the summer
a seamless surround of insect song
like a wave poised above
the house, never breaking.
My mother on the couch.
The book in her lap
might be *Dr. Zhivago*
(I remember the white cover)
or *Under the Greenwood Tree.*
Hardy was her favorite
so I'm sure I saved that one.
The moths throwing themselves
at the brass table lamp.
The later it got, the bigger
the moths, and the louder
their furred, frantic bodies
seeking the light.

We walked slowly, thoughtfully
as he puffed the last of his cigar.
Then the winding brick path
and the penetrating scent of yew,
musty and fertile, as if all the arching trees
and hedges were mulched with books.
My father would hoist me
onto the serpentine wall
so I could jig and crow and look down
on his tonsured pate.
Inside was Hannah Severn, saintly
Quaker librarian, and all around her
circulation desk, jackets whispering
floorboards creaking respectfully.
Here we parted ways—my father
to the American History mezzanine
and I, to Juvenile Fiction.
We stayed for ages, the whole town
In there with us, sunk in bookish bliss.
Then the 8:30 gong and my grubby
tattered card offered up.
The walk home
a fresh cigar
our arms amiably full.

Mr. Wesolowski,
ex-Marine, part-time cop
and our town's swimming instructor
is yelling his head off.
Which one of us chicken-skinny
five-year-olds, hypnotized
by gleaming, slappy water
we know to be over our heads
has made Mr. Wesolowski so mad?
I have not understood
a single thing since I got here.
Now he is blowing a silver whistle
so, like a rabbit darting into the open
I jump—and in my airborne moment,
see my mother rise to her feet.

I go down a long way
in my own plume of white.
How quiet and capacious
this big blue room
and how little used,
like a church during the week.
Surprising, how I rise
without even trying, and then
not much of a surprise
am pulled up and out
by Mr. Wesolowski
and set on the pool's
rough, concrete lip
knowing for certain now
he is yelling at me.

OLD FLAME

Thirty-six years have passed
and I get jealous just reading a poem
about a man who might be you.
One of your ex-es is visiting—
it's her poem—and patience is required
on her part; you are restrained
and sad. It could easily be you.
An island in Maine, an old
Chevy pick-up, raspberries,
blackberries, and blueberries
ripening at the same time
all of us wading into the August
woods with buckets, bowls, and jars
anything we could fill.
The man in the poem likes cats
Which, as I recall, you did.
And he's been married five times.
There would have been time for that.
Now you and this ex-wife
or girlfriend are walking together
through the hemlocks
on the north side of the island
and she is taking everything in:
The narrow path down to the water
the apple-green garter snake
looping suddenly out of the tall grass
the rowboat you use for trips to town.

Now I remember how it was:
Me unfolding like a one-page letter
you touching a match to one corner
all the words burning away, everything
turning to the thinnest, lightest ash.

I'll wait by the door.
I'll be wearing a long, black
coat and grey mittens.
I'll have brown hair—
medium brown, medium long.
I'll be the medium girl
with a notebook and a pen.
I'll be the skinny girl
in glasses and cut-off jeans.
I'll be the wallflower
waiting by the door,
the girl in a white, sleeveless
blouse to whom nothing happens.
I'll be empty-handed
except for the notebook.
I'll be the one who did it
on the bleachers, on a bed of moss
and under the old apple tree.
I'll be waiting by the door
wearing bird and star earrings
I found in a thrift store
and I'll have auburn hair.
I'll be holding a small
child by the hand
and I'll look as though
I've seen a ghost.
I'll be so bundled up
in my long black coat
you won't recognize me.
I'll be carrying a notebook
and I'll be waiting by the door.

POEM BEGINNING WITH A LINE BY GERALD STERN

The weeds give up suddenly, after a small struggle
a flat metal strip, rusted just
the color of the native dirt
and enmeshed in the fine white root
of clover, now in bloom here.
I bend to brush it clean
and straightening, see
its ghost, a pale shape
where the garage door lost a hinge
seasons and years and lives ago.

HOME

I tell everybody I'm not from here.
I grew up in a little leafy town
an Avalon, really, two day's
hard rowing from Cleveland.
Tonight when I leave work,
it's dark, and the parking lot
on Euclid Avenue has emptied.
Passing cars spotlight dead weeds
caught in the chain link fence
and now, falling past
these rooms of light is snow.
Snow circles me as I find
the car door lock with my key.
A man calls through the snow
to his son, "Over here, Immani
come over here, where I can see you."
The boy, mitten dangling
stands still, and I stand next to him
stunned by the snow
then flattened by a sudden gigantic
gnashing, roaring, vibration—
a locomotive passing
on the 116th-street bridge
and disappearing into the billowing snow.
It's almost as if an elk
or a bighorn sheep
has clattered across my path
so intent in his own business
that I might belong here, too;
this might be home.

BLOOD SHOULD BE THICKER THAN THIS

It was so good to see you,
I say, on the heels
of your annual visit
and I really mean it, but
I wish I could just drop in
maybe help with the dishes
snap green beans.
We could talk or not.
You could show me the new family room
describe how the electrician
showed up every other week.

Or you could come over here.
We'd take a walk and you'd end up
staying for dinner, and then
we'd all watch *My Cousin Vinny,*
and it would be like Mass
because we know all the lines
and we'd be saying them together.

It *was* a nice visit.
You asked me what was new.
I showed you my shoebox crown
and you listened to the whole story.
Maybe I went on too long
I thought you got a little restless.
Still, when I dropped you at the airport
I felt the fabric tearing.

THIS COULD BE TRUE

I just had the most wonderful dream.
We were all somewhere really great—
not here—but wherever it was—
we all belonged there.
It was summer—we were all barefoot
out in the street, and I think we were dancing.
There were no cars, no streetlights,
but it was very bright where we all were.
It was just getting dark,
and all the stores were wide open
glowing inside with a warm, buttery light
against a deep blue-black, stacked-up sky.

We must have been near the water
because I could smell it.
The night air must have been
bringing the smell of the water inland.
Red and green and yellow lanterns
were strung on the phone lines,
and there were white lights
out on the water, shimmering.

And then you came dancing
through the crowd,
both arms in the air.
You were wearing that aqua
blue dress you have
with the white vines and flowers
and you were shouting, "I told you!
Remember, how I said you should
have more fun? Wasn't I right?
You gave me a big strong hug,
and I felt the pressure of it on my ribs
a long time after I woke up.

LOREN WEISS
2006 CLEVELAND HEIGHTS POET LAUREATE

A former president of both the American Die Casting Institute and Oakwood Country Club, Loren Weiss has a background in mechanical engineering and played varsity golf while a student at the University of Wisconsin and the University of Louisville. He worked in the die casting industry for more than 40 years and has been a certified pilot since 1970. He has been married to his wife, Lita, for 54 years.

Loren's publications include a self-published poetry collection called *I'd Rather Be Flying* and poems in *Ohioana Library, Ohio Writer, Tributaries*, and *Palo Alto Review*.

THOUGHTS ABOUT MY POET LAUREATE EXPERIENCE
Loren Weiss

It was one of the important events of my eightieth year, to attend the May 2006 City Council meeting, where (thanks to Heights Arts), they appointed me Poet Laureate of Cleveland Heights.

I accepted the assignment: to promote the art of poetry in the community, especially by presenting poems at important civic functions.

I soon learned about the challenge to write a poem on demand, about a specific event. This is 180 degrees from writing to express a feeling or emotion that has surfaced in the course of daily life.

A little like writing an essay, first the subject has to be researched. Then the creative juices have to be filtered for how to hook the reader.

My assignment in June of 2006, was to compose a poem to be read at one of the gardens on the Summer Solstice Garden Tour. This was a fundraiser for The Heights Youth Club, to renovate and make an activities home for them out of the Church at the corner of Washington Blvd. and Lee Rd. My poem, "A Chance to Grow," was enthusiastically received and published in the tour guide.

In September 2006, I composed and presented the poem, "A New Link," at the dedication of the renovated main Cleveland Heights-University Heights library on Lee Road. It was so well received by the staff, a framed calligraphy copy was created. It now hangs on the wall near the entrance to the office area on the first floor. What a thrill to be so recognized!

The highlight of my term, was reading to the large audience at Cain Park on the recognition night for CH volunteers. As I came off stage, Viktor Schreckengost, who was waiting there to be recognized on the occasion of his 100th birthday, looked up at me from his wheelchair, took my eighty-year-old hand, and said "Very nice, young man."

Thanks again for having me as your Poet Laureate.

Sometimes it doesn't take much
to put me to sleep
at Severance Hall.
Tonight it's Gustave Mahler,
Symphony Number Five.
Music full of heavy brass chords,
Trumpets, horns, trombones
unleashed in all their polished glory.
Strings play feverishly to be heard,
try not to be forgotten.
Glorious music flows,
ebbs, engulfs me
in rich sonorous waves
that break over me.
I struggle to stay afloat.
Think about my friend for life,
or try to compose a poem.
It works.
Awake still
when the music ends,
I did not drown in sleep.
Bravo!
Thunderous applause....
Could some be for me?

Witold Lutoslawski Symphony No. 4

Atonal garbage grows
on stage in rows
at Severance Hall.
Periods of unexplained silence
fester between measures,
seem to fill with swirling gas.
At the end
a final chord...
a huge fart.

Sun is up, air is warm.
I sit on the screened back porch,
sip black coffee.
Look out at the green expanse of lawn
freshened by yesterday's thunderstorms.
Border of tall majestic pin-oak
creates shelter from wind,
filters out hazy sun.
Two rabbits chase back and forth.
He pretends to munch grass,
edges carefully up behind.
Suddenly he springs toward her,
she jumps into the air
and escapes.
The scene repeats itself.
Hey Mr. Cottontail,
I know what you're doing
you lucky bastard. Why not
try to kiss her first?
That usually works for me.
I watch... I become embarrassed.
Somewhere in thick bushes,
a few children of this union
will be born. Somehow hide them,
protect them from raccoons, skunks,
neighbors cats and dogs
that wander through. Let
live so someday there will be
another pair of you for me
to watch as I drink black coffee
on my screened back porch.

COFFEE BREAK

Early October, Sunday afternoon
sun at my back, caresses me.
Black coffee balances on
bench seat's wide iron straps,
waits its turn to warm me inside.
Young couple sits opposite,
can't make contact, eyes
hidden behind sunglasses.
They nurse latte from
slotted top Styrofoam cups.
Subdued talk passes
between sips, and quiet smiles.
Muscle shirt exposes bronzed bare arms
resting against her matching tan.
Toe to shoulder, they are
pressed against each other.
Sun sinks below red bricks.
In shadows now, they rise,
hands locked, stroll off,
perhaps to find sunlight
in a corner of his bedroom.

SIXTIETH REUNION, 2004

Thin gray hair
covers heads bent forward
awkwardly trying to read
name tags thru bifocals,
a check for survivors.
Those we hardly knew
in nineteen forty-four,
become new best friends.
Find Elaine. Finally
time to tell her
how I loved her silently,
in grades seven,
eight, and nine.

Pressed against each other,
hug held. Soft and warm,
lips brush slowly, briefly,
sixty years late.

SNACK TIME

Sit on a green wooden bench,
feet propped up on metal railing.
Crowded beach below the pier
stretches out toward Malibu
as far as the eye can see.
Old man with sun-baked face and
head of salt and pepper curls, nods,
joins me. Without speaking, reaches
into crumpled plastic bag filled
with Cheetos. Picks one out,
holds aloft in weather-beaten fingers.
A white seagull making lazy circles,
arcs down toward us.
Without stopping, snaps crispy orange
snack in yellow beak, eats it in flight.
Four gray gulls follow, descend to
sit on railing, anxiously eye the old man.
Screes beg in vain for their turn.
He ignores them, hoists another morsel.
The white gull reappears from nowhere,
swoops in, snatches another Cheeto,
is gone before the others
can get airborne. As the scene repeats,
old man turns to me. "He knows me.
I feed that bird every day."
Soon he responds to the
pleading gray gulls, tosses Cheetos
they grab in mid-air.
I love Cheetos.
I wonder, if I ask, will he
reach into that bottomless supply
to let me have one too?

ERIE ROCKS AND ROLLS

The lake, like an ocean, stretches out
as far as the eye can see. Northwind howls.
Waves smash against the break wall,
pulverized water sprays toward angular gleaming glass.

Inside the crystal pyramid, silence...
Guitars line walls, hang patiently
in tribute to their legends, await in vain
their turn to be heard above the wind.

Ride the old ferry-boat.
Roll with waves
from strong northeast wind.
Ten miles ahead
lies inviting green island.
Slender shaft made of
majestic marble blocks,
visible for over twenty miles,
rises four hundred feet
above the tree covered mass
of glacier scarred limestone....
Monument to brave souls
lost in the battle of Lake Erie
almost two hundred years ago.
Decks awash then,
with red blood of
both sides young men
spilled into Erie's blue-green water.
Wasted...
No one won that war.

LI RIVER

Boats in single file,
a giant Chinese dragon,
drifting snake-like
through the seductive scene.
Flotilla of Peking ducks
guards the pebbled shore.
Horned, bestial, water buffalo
play submarine, dive to graze
on seaweed covered river-bed.
Peaks materialize, phantoms
out of the blue-gray haze ahead.
Either side, karst mountains, lush,
green shrouded, rise up out of the earth
through shards of sifting mist.
Imagination time....
A camel, a horse, a bearded old man.
A field of mounds topped off
with points, erect nipples
of naked women.
Sharply outlined, tree covered,
vertical, a phallic shape pierces fog
that settles around it,
fades into firmament behind.
Chinese dragon rides the sensuous flow.

Don't even think about
how far there is to go.
Count twenty-five stone steps,
uneven, stop for rest...
repeat, repeat...
negotiate with God
to survive the climb.
Throngs of olive eyed
jabber, babble, push
upward from behind.
Swarms circle around.
Thighs ache, breath comes
in deep hard draughts,
sweat soaks my clothes
under the Gortex wind shell.
Through lookout windows
in the sides of the endless
great stone monster, cold wind
whips at my wet head and neck.
chills my overheated blood.
Sharply upward,
last two hundred feet,
legs turn to jelly, barely walking.
Cling to the hand rail.
Don't yield, then
finally, a level place.
Rest period, look down.
How did they build it
over twenty-two centuries ago,
four thousand miles
across jagged mountain tops?
Hundreds of thousands,
sweated more than I,
couldn't stop for rest.
So many died. Still lying
packed in with sticky rice
somewhere underneath me.

A Chance to Grow

Look out at lawns,
green, refreshed by Spring.
Dandelions blossom...
golden, full of promise,
fight for space to call their own.
Unobstructed, they grow wild,
choke out opposition,
whatever is in their way.
Bright blossoms burn out
quickly, turn to flimsy fuzz,
blow away to plant
destructive seeds somewhere else.
Without love, unattended, kids
spring up like wild flowers.
Need a fertile garden, a place to grow.
Protected space, a place
to learn respect for what it takes
to grow tall like the steeple
at Washington Blvd. and Lee Rd.
Learn too, they are not alone.
Firmly anchored together,
withstand the storms of growing.
And in time, be there
for the golden harvest.

Hi Mom

Walk on the crunchy gravel drive.
Look over the hedge at the garden,
sun's rays over my shoulder, shining
on a cosmos with perfect pink petals.
Its single yellow-gold eye
looks directly at me.
I smile...the flower smiles back.
Touched by that magic,
what if some of those we've loved
come back as beautiful flowers,
so they can feel our love again?
My mother always planted comos
until she died in nineteen fifty one.
I smile again at the flower.
Air is calm, yet it nods.
And then...it smiles back.

SWEET SIXTEEN

I have seen the laughter
in her eyes.
Warm blue eyes
with deep blue laughter
born of innocence.
Makes men wonder
how they'll ever
love another after
time and vanity erase
the deep blue laughter,
leave in its place,
the cool grey mist
of conquest
and deceitful lies.

CRUSHED

Sit patiently in a parking lot exit,
wait for oncoming traffic to clear.
Relentlessly, wet snow falls, covers pavement.
Slush for salty snow cones accumulates.
An '89 gas guzzler,
black and chrome,
approaches from the left,
tries to turn in. It slides...
in slow motion, right front bumper
implants itself in my left front fender.

Tall, young, blond and beautiful,
driver gives me her insurance info.
It assures me she's in good hands,
State Farm will take care of everything.
Her name vibrates a brain cell.
Curious writer within me
asks her where she works.
"Associate Editor *Northern Ohio Live*"
Wow!
I've met an editor
without an appointment.
I send her a copy of this poem.
My car lives.
The poem dies
in her slush pile.

PROFILED

A thunderstorm in progress
over Denver Airport,
has the airspace closed.
Waiting for delayed flights,
anxious people fidget,
crowd into aisles
with blue plastic seats.
A swarthy man,
head shaved and polished,
sits two rows away, facing me.
Eyes set in deep dark sockets
behind wire-rimmed glasses,
refuse contact, stare at nothing.
Black moustache trimmed
in a thin line, extends down
along each side of his mouth,
joins the beard looping
around under sullen lips.
He doesn't notice
the young man
sitting next to me,
sketching him.
What's in his pockets.
I wonder.
My flight is called.
No sweat.
He's not boarding.

January Lake Effect

Daily weather-maps say
Winter has us by the icicles,
no letting go any time soon.
Frequent, innocent snow showers
fall, relentlessly build
giant white toadstools,
over-hanging hats on shrubs.
Trucks spread salt,
turn road surfaces into slush.
Cars splatter each other,
coat with splotches
of corrosive residue.
Feel it rusting holes,
in the doors...the fenders.
Snow plows roam streets,
wart hogs looking
for giant Slurpies to feed on.
Hot air from the President
(State of the Union speech)
doesn't help.
January thaw has been
postponed by Lake Erie.

Big Fish Adventure: Part I

Six hundred miles
due North of Saskatoon,
the boisterous groan of the
old radial engine, turns mellow,
as Luc powers back, trims,
sets the DeHavilland gently
on the pure, glass-like surface.
Our destination comes into view,
mirrored on calm water.
Rustic cabins, freshly varnished,
glisten, nestled among island's trees
in the middle of Scott Lake.
Gear unloaded (except for Jeff's),
quickly delivered to cabin Wolf,
our home for next five days.
Jeff rushes around, cabin to dock
to cabin. Shouts ring out
in pristine evening air,
"Where the fuck is my luggage!"
I unpack. My brother Howard
spreads treasure on the table.
Carefully selected, purchased in Saskatoon,
four hundred dollars in Cuban cigars,
to be divvied up, smoked with relish,
after dinners and shore lunches.
Jeff calms. His gear has surfaced,
somehow delivered by mistake to a lodge
ninety wilderness miles to the east,
to be flown in by tomorrow breakfast.
Cool crisp night descends after dinner.
We bond with other guests around camp-fire
outside the main hall. Eyes search the
now dark sky, disappointed at faint glow
of Aurora Borealis. Big fish
will make a better show tomorrow.

Big Fish Adventure: Part II

Rod tip barely bobbles.
A tentative tug on the line?
Hoist the rod tip sharply up
NOW!...to set the hook...
A tug...
Then harder, a tug, tug, tug.
Start to wind...
Unexpected, rod bends,
to the strength of the fish,
flexes beyond a right angle.
Tip held high now, a cushion,
or the unseen captive
will break the line,
swim away to freedom.
Tugging stops...
Careful, it may be
swimming toward the rod.
Wind quickly, keep tension on the line.
If it goes slack, the prize will be gone,
without swirl or flash of belly white,
no open jaws breaking surface plane.
Oh no... line is taught, no tugging.
Shit...maybe I've snagged bottom.
Suddenly, fight resumes.
It's not bottom after all.
It's one goddamn big fish.
The struggle feels familiar.
Was it at birth
while still connected...
the unspoken lure of fishing?
Finally, held up out of water,
then released from the hook alive,
we both will remember this meeting.
My pleasure is in that feeling,
not in killing the fish.

SMALL TOWN DESSERT

A warm May dusk,
walk among happy throngs,
cruise Main Street, smile
as you approach the antique
ice-cream popcorn parlor
clinging to the shale hillside.
Little kids ride dad's shoulders,
big dogs strain on tight leashes.
Young men, old men,
steal furtive glances at tan midriffs
inset with sparkly crystal.
Walk down the winding wooden stairs,
watch Chagrin's river swollen
over its banks by yesterday's
thunderous downpour. Roaring
like Niagara, falls drown out
the tuba and accordion
upstairs on the sidewalk
playing "Roll Out the Barrel."
Customers, satisfied, eagerly lick
chocolate or vanilla frozen custard.
Convertibles roll slowly past
showing off blond hair
splayed on bare shoulders.
Sensuous, pervading the
deepening early eve.

Time to Remember

It stands in quiet dignity, set back from Mayfield,
surrounded by green, not far from Cumberland.
Four sides covered,
familiar names on glass covered plaques.
I count them. Cleveland Heights
sent five-thousand, eight-hundred-
and-fifty lives to WWII.
Stars mark one-hundred-and-fifty-six,
couldn't come back to read their names.
Nearby, beige marble blocks set in red brick,
engraved with eleven who died in Vietnam,
twelve lost in Korea.
Similar structures in other communities
have the same mission.
The ultimate, in black marble, stretches out
in the shadow of Lincoln's memorial.
Loved ones journey to D.C. to touch,
names carved into shining stone,
names at rest forever.
More are dying now on unfriendly desert sand.
Will we need to build some more?
We better get started soon.

TRAPPED

I sit in my office,
the buzz, thump, and hum
of the factory turned off.
Welcome silence.
Swivel toward the window
where a month ago
I squeezed the life out of
a spider roaming innocently
between two Plexiglas panels,
strategically placed
to soften Winter's breath..
Its lifeless body pressed now
with legs outstretched
in silhouette against
opaque sky beyond...
We take our chances
every day. How easily
we can be caught,
entrapped...
hurt feelings on display.

TOMORROW

Smoke snakes up into blue haze
from half dead butts that sprawl
in a maze of lips and hands.....
Other lips and hands caress a glass.
Drink up, so long
as another guy pays.
Other lips demand a drink.
The jukebox plays
loud through the stink,
the smell of sin-bought sorrow.
Words lose meaning,
lips have to drink.
Jukebox plays too loud to think.
Nobody here gives a damn....
about tomorrow.

EXAM TIME

Stripped naked, I note the suit I was born in.
It's wrinkled, where
once it was smooth and nicely filled.
Covered lightly now, with thin cotton gown
tied up the back, still partly open.
Lie on fresh white paper,
on top of a hard table
that moves on rollers.
Slide into the huge plastic doughnut.
Lights chase each other around
in a circular clear glass inner raceway.
It purrs with soft cat-like sounds.
"Hold your breath now"......
Freeze for a few moments,
on the edge of a silent hurricane.
Then pass through the eye of the storm
into the clear beyond.
The end of the scan
by the one CAT
to which I'm not allergic.

REMISSION

Words roll off the doctor's tongue,
like a waiter confirming
my dinner order. "You have
a blood lymphoma...a cancer
not curable, but treatable,
when your blood chemistry
tells me its time."
Three years later,
stretched out on a La-Z-Boy,
trade first names with Karen.
We drift into our own thoughts,
not caring to intrude
on each other's hazy episode.
Look up at clear bag of fluid
hooked on arms of
shiny stainless stick-man
towering above me.
Clear liquid drips,
from clear plastic pouch,
thru clear plastic valve, into
clear plastic spaghetti,
its needle nose stuck
into an innocent blue vein.
Around the room,
La-Z-Boys aligned
in a semi-circle,
like ladies under dryers
at a beauty parlor.
Five of us similarly hooked,
soak up our medicine,
seek our Holy Grail...

GRAVEYARD

When I ran the business
all by myself
(after my partner was
out of it), I learned
it was pretty lonely at the top.
In the plant,
late afternoon sun
filters in thru sooty windows,
casts long shadows
on unlit work-weathered floor.
A few presses remain,
sold for pennies on the dollar,
wait to be lifted from their old home,
strapped on a flat-bed
to be scrapped, to be dead.
Until then they stand there,
obelisks in a graveyard.
So guess what?
It's pretty fucking lonely
at the bottom, too....

No Way Out

For those inside,
the exit from Hell
is always just ahead,
blocked by a pile
of broken rocks,
Devil's pitch fork,
a tool to freedom.
The door, uncovered,
will open. Beyond it?
Just another pile of rocks.
That's the Hell of it

The cordless phone on my desk
rings, jars me awake.
It's Amy, asking the
Poet Laureate from HeightsWrites
to compose a piece
to kick off a special event,
the high school poetry slam.
No sweat, I think. Then
I stare at the blank screen,
an empty Word document.
The only thing I see
on the cold white glass,
(a forecast of an early snow,)
is a spot from a recent sneeze.
Not the inspiration I'm looking for.
But then that moisture starts me thinking.
Hmm...If I can write a poem
about writing poetry, it
will be about the poets...
how they yearn and suffer,
their need to expose feelings,
to set minds at peace.
So tell them to write
how the smell of a face
brings back the taste of
that first wet kiss, of
tongues tentatively touching...
and then the long wait until
it happens again,
tomorrow...
That's stuff
young poets' poems
can be made of.

LOSER

I like to wager
when the chance to win
can be calculated.
I know,
there is also a chance
to lose.
Horse favored to win
by all the experts
doesn't feel like running today,
can't tell us why.
Black comes up
ten times in a row
on the roulette wheel.
Now....
Bet the bundle on Red.
Ball skitters and bounces.
Sure enough, it's not Black.
This time it drops in......
the slot for Zero,
the color of unripe tomatoes.
The ultimate gamble
is to fall in love.
When all signs say go ahead,
proceed with loving caution.
Horse didn't tell you
if he felt like running.
Sure bet on Red
turned sour Green.

MARY E. WEEMS
2007 & 2008 CLEVELAND HEIGHTS POET LAUREATE

Mary E. Weems is a nationally known writer, performer, and educator. She is currently on the faculty of John Carroll University in University Heights, Ohio. Having written poetry for forty years and performed poetry for almost as long, Mary brings to her work as an educator years of experience tailoring the written word to an audience.

Mary's publications include an educational book called *Publication and the Imagination-Intellect: I Speak from the Wound in my Mouth* (Peter Lang 2003) and several poetry collections, including *An Unmistakable Shade of Red and The Obama Chronicles* (Bottom Dog Press 2008), *Tampon Class* (Pavement Saw Press 2005), and *White* (Wick 1997). Mary's poems have appeared in many publications. Mary has also served as editor on two other poetry anthologies, *Cleveland Poetry Scenes: A Panorama & Anthology* (Bottom Dog Press 2008) and *Working Hard for the Money: America's Working Poor in Stories, Poems, and Photos* (Bottom Dog Press 2002).

HA! POET LAUREATE
Mary E. Weems

To this day, when someone points out that I'm the current poet laureate I look around to see who they're talking about. This title takes me back to my Greek mythology class at CSU, the professor a lover of words expressed as gods, goddesses and battles stretched his requirements to let me do Byron's "She Walks in Beauty" as a rap—Flava Flav clock around my neck, baseball cap turned like a top—me excited, trying not to lose my composure between end rhymes. I remember the day the committee interviewed me at the Studio, Loren and Meredith sending good vibes my way as I was questioned about poetry, my love for it and what I'd do if selected laureate. It's been one helluva going on two years—meeting the mayor, council and his administrative staff, reading to the gracious seniors at the Community Center, reciting before the play at Cain park last summer, sharing poetry at Cleveland Heights High School.

Working as part of an established committee of folks dedicating volunteer time to the arts they love has been joyful—our Joy of Text performance still giving me thoughtful chuckles when I remember some of the carefully constructed lines Bunny found about the beginning of the written word.

My one big project during this tenure was using poetry to build community by asking CH-UH residents to visit local book stores and libraries and invite a partner (preferably someone they didn't know) to create Found Poems with. Although the working with a stranger component bombed like a bad joke on amateur night at a comedy club, the people who did participate shared some incredible found poems, including my friend Kat Blackbird, who picked up on the Found Poetry project and had some of her students create poems they shared at Heights Arts Studio. A few weeks later, with Peggy's loan of a brown paper bag of "This is Where" lines written by community members coinciding with places on the hand-drawn map of Cleveland Heights—I found community and created a found poem with selected "bag" lines titled "Opening the Lines of Communication."

Now that I've lived in Cleveland Heights for several years, I understand why so many of my friends who've lived out here for much longer—love this community. There's a lot to celebrate—and I'll never run out of things to write poems about.

It's been a wonderful, blessed, nurturing ride—thank you.
Peace.

Nature Haiku

Truck Stop. Picnic Table.
Trees stand like giants in drag.
Flock of butterflies.

Styrofoam. Dogs walk
in woods sans owners. Won't even
take a pee on it.

Grand Canyon is an
open mouth. She whispers
Get out don't come back.

River lay on her back
an unwilling prostitute.
Pollution, her pimp.

Harvest Moon
For Masumi Hayashi

Tonight the moon
is the sun, a gold poem, Masumi's
face.

She sits in the just-night sky
close to her old ways
aims her lens
watches the new hollow hole
the world is from the outside
in

one thousand years it will still
be that day coming back to repeat
itself like senseless violence
in the street

like sudden murder in a safe house

like the wail yesterday is.

Mama Haiku
For Adah

When you lose your mom
to transition, the hole in
your navel closes.

Sunset. Mama's not
speaking to me, but I hear
her voice when I do.

ON ALMOST MEETING ALICE WALKER
12-7-07

She is stature-small, wears the universe
and comfortable shoes. Center stage,
the ancestors dance around her like the fire
next time, their spirits the light coming
from the ceiling, the voices that echo
when the distance-learning children
ask their questions.

I am listening to the white and black people
address her as Alice, wondering if they think
they are lost in the looking glass
of a fairy tale where respect disappears
in the drink that takes that Alice
to the Mad Hatter.

In the live audience, all
of us reach for her breath; a wisdom
of purple, solitude, and love
slowly reversing evil, one word at a time;
like a water drop on a mountain
timeless, and as much a part of the world
as her wire rimmed glasses, her poignant
morality, a wildflower—unbowed.

CHINA LOVE NOTES

China shifts like a grave.
Brave people pretend it's over
help tomorrow come.

Day and night names drop
from why? One man walks miles arms
open for missing son.

There is no coffin
large enough. Thousands of faces look
away from yesterday.

Countryside. Death's long
line. People from every country
wait. Carry another.

World is on its knees.
Prayers, chants, soft-spoken words.
One language—love.

In America, Spring
turns to winter wears
mourning weeds, hides.

This morning a green
shoot pushed through a broken cup—
a child's small smile.

FOUND POEM

A woman is dying for want of a single, unrealized
word—freedom

America's rotting rib cage frames the gallows
of her putrid goals.

The young vomit and turn away,
America becomes a bloated corpse.

Alone to my bed, where *I love you*
is on touching tongues, silent in their meeting,
her name is sewn along the edges of my dreams.

There are no bottoms to words, like the reefs,
when we ourselves have died, they are the skeletons of our life work.

Sapphire lizards send fire
and I burn for centuries unborn.

[Found in *The Hand That Cradles the Rock* by Rita Mae Brown, pp. 23,
24, 28, 36, 37, 38, 45. Two words were added: they, are (L11).]

Snap Shot

everybody's blood
blood baths
8 pints between life and death
war and hope

politicians talk about Hope
for the *free* world
people wave flags
sons and daughters on the front line

Hope is the end of the tunnel
the first night no one dies
skin color subtitle
all of the battlefields the same:
heads, arms, legs like loose change,
no common ground, ammo shells,

a beautiful, sunlit sky.

[Inspired by Lilian Tyrrell, Weaving, *Abandoned Heroes*, 1993]

MAKE SOME NOISE

Marcelle Marceau
silence art
white over white
face stay-young
eye on re-creation
sound as motion

Met his magic
black and white screen
small, eye squint

Believed disguise
performance, Morse code,
clarified humanity
unexpected as a 50-dollar bill
in a street mime's hat.

Baby? Girl you know long I been tryin' to find you? I can't
believe I'm finally hearing your voice. Listen, I can't talk long
but daddy wants to give you his overseas phone number—yeah,
I'm leaving soon as I get off the phone—won't be back for at least
a year maybe....daughter, baby girl?

Pops! Yeah, I got the money—thanks for sending it right
away...yeah,
I know you told me to stay away from Snake, naw he still don't give
extra time to pay—hell naw he don't care what your problems are
he's a no-long-story, I don't play that person...Huh? No, I don't
know where I'm gettin' next week's payment. (PAUSE) Okay, I
know you've heard this story one time to many...the real deal is....

Heeeeeeeelp! Police, Police, yes, this me, I mean you don't me, I
mean my name
is Mary, what? What difference do my last name make—oh, shit,
helllllllp please, stop! Tommy, get your ass——Police, my name is
Mary, I live at 15503 Lake—

(Whispering) Hello ma? How are you doing? No, it hasn't—I called
you last Mother's Day remember? Yep, I sent the roses—sorry, they
were supposed to send red, not white
no I wasn't trying to be funny—what could be "funny" about you
being dead? Yeah, I'll try for Christmas again this year. You know
how it is—holidays are when overtime at the CIA is mandatory—
Where will I be next week? Moscow, mama—phones are funny over
there. Huh? You want the number anyway? Yeah, I can wait until
you get a pencil Mama wait a minute ma?
Duuuuuuuuuuuuuuuuunnnnnnn.

[Inspired by Lilian Tyrrell, Weaving, *Loss of Communication*, 1988]

YOUNG MAN WITH NO LEGS
For Bobby Martin

What's he doing
standing in eyes
sky tall, star gazing
straight as if future is light
aware everywhere

Black man walks time
each day another chance at chance
his smile last time I saw moon
as a man

I feel a gentle touch
Humble rests on lashes
wet with this gift
a glance at hope.

Bobby Pins

She drinks to go back.
Pushes rewind on spirit,
drops through Blackland
to Alice's hole. The think
in the drink: dreams
blurred, one-jump rope,
little pressed bobby pinned curls.

A shade darker, few years
earlier, she could be me
on the other side, never
a child, I looked the part,
insides a mama-made
mama, 3 kids watched
while she drank to go back
too.

What's new is my own
dreams, nightmares
of woman-too-soon
long cantchy-dontchy,
rope-thick braids,
change to grownup
curls at twelve,
the period that came
with a mama who said
take this and go
in the bathroom.

I used to drink,
look down her hole,
unfamiliar as Black dolls
in the 50s, the entry blocked
by a door only a child's
bobby pin could open.

PLAYING BARBIE
(A True Story)

I see Barbie (who doesn't really move)
come to the door of her pink, pre-packaged
Barbie Doll House.

Pink is everywhere. Down-pink bed sprinkled
with sky. Ceiling, pink universe. Jane
and Jane sit on floor short-bobbed, manicured,
big brains, playing Barbie—No Ken.

It's Jane's turn. She brushes flaxen
filaments, tries on her big-enough-for-little-girl
earrings, puts teeny pink lips on her mouth.

Jane wait-watches.
Jane tells Jane to go home.
Jane won't go without Barbie.
The room rains pink.
It wets Barbie's hair.
It starts to stink.
See Jane snatch Barbie.
See Jane slap Jane.
Jane goes without Barbie.
Jane laughs.
Barbie is dancing.

Hear Jane holler outside.
Jane laughs inside
opens her door.

See Barbie walk Jane home.
Steak knife is red.
Jane is red.

THE HOLE IN THE WALL

is a dark star
cut into, faces brick
like a punished child.

Inside the star is wild
a mosh of objects
disorganized as thought on crank:
cigarettes butts bent
by same lip
small shoes with no right feet
unopened letters from strangers
brown beer bottles stacked as soldiers marching
hats off
heads missing

toy missiles in the air point
to tomorrow
permanently tipped
in stranger-in-a-strange-land blood

The whole world this space
a song un-played
the lyrics caught
like a voyeur
inside a just-occupied
room.

THE STORY OF MARRIAGE
For James

Tanka
This was their happy.
The stone reads my eyes.
She reaches from the ground,
tells me the story of marriage
in exactly thirty-one breaths.

Third Finger
You wear a size 15!?
Jeweler says, sizes stop at 12.
You swallow my hand
I feel your left palm years later
when it is old and wrinkled.

Wedding Day
The Limo is white.
We are groomed and on time
Graceland waits like love.
We embrace the minister,
dine at the top of the world.

Love Note
When I look into your eye
the other one opens lightly
its brown becomes our river
where I swim in you naked
searching for the road not taken.

Wedding Night
There is only one night
vibrating with single stars.
We name each one *joy,*
dance on the dark of the sky
memorize our light two-step.

Morning Tanka
The back of your head
rushing out of our driveway
highlights ears shaped
like the coffee cup you left
half gulped on my moist back.

Footnote
All of the drawers
and doors you opened watch.
I follow your steps.
Mumbling about messiness
I caress each place you left.

Anger
When the clock strikes one
we say more than we mean. Hurt,
you leave without eyes.
Home before the clock reads two,
we say what we mean together.

Dessert
My sweet tooth's a tongue
licking the crumbs from cakes quick
hidden like secrets
in places in our kitchen your
hand has made easy to find.

Rescue
My car sits alone
in the lot like a left child
your truck is a steed
I carry poems from the kids
read them as you change the tire.

Breast Food
Inside I practice
living alone in Death's house.
I say *I'm not afraid,*
you sit staring still as stone.
your sudden tears on my t-shirt.

Heartbeat
I walk to your bed
holding my own hand. You start
ask *Are you alright?*
I rush to answer: My lips
kiss your smile, my eyes flowers.

Recitation
Your secret desire
spills from your mouth in a dream.
Asleep you recite
McKay's "If we must die" and
the audience applauds forever.

Haiku
We die with our eyes
open because we want to see
where we go next.

DANCE LESSON
William H. Johnson, *Soldiers Dancing*, 1942

"Dance with me, come on dance
with me baby, dance with me..."

Plays on the phonograph
the song out of place in World War II

Two brown-dressed Nazis
with huge white hands grip
each woman like fear. Marvin Gaye,
time traveler, watches from the
stale ceiling air

as they step on bound feet,
stare into brown-not-blue eyes.

A look of surprise when the music stops
and they keep the women spinning,
stumbling

breaking the heels of their shoes
wetting the floor
staining the hems
of their dresses.

THE KISS

I see two trees
and it's the end of World War II
in a black and white movie.

Nothing rhymes with freedom
in the cadence of dark soldiers returning
for another shot at the their forty acres
and a mule. There is a march from madness
back to a U.S. that welcomes white soldiers
with one hand, begins putting new locks
on doors to make Black heroes knock over
and over like jokes to no answers
with the other.

Standing at the base of these two trees
kissing like the lovers in that image,
I wonder what they were like at the end of the war
when these woods were young.

If their dark brown barks are the reason
they hold each other so tightly.

"MINER AT REST"
Irwin Hoffman, 1939

The lit cigarette in his right
drop-dead-tired-hand
is the only thing holding
him up—the hot tip more
fire than his heart dipped
in coal dust so long
it pumps black.

He doesn't remember when
he wasn't a miner walking to
work with his Dad as soon as
he could carry the lunch bucket
collecting loose lumps from the
ground like coins.

At night he'd hold his short pants
up, help his Dad home from the
only pub in town—beer-guzzled,
grizzled, mumbling about pots of
gold and the little green men
following them home.

He dropped out of high school
the last time his teacher held
her nose in her eyes asking
what day of the week he was
allowed to bathe.

Her face is a blank, but her words
are carved into his chest, an unwelcome
tattoo beating dark and slow
waiting for the end of his shift.

"PASTORAL PUERTO RICO"
Irwin Hoffman, 1939

They are the land—
brown, strong, re-worked.
They move one motion—hoe-to-soil,
hoe-to-soil, wipe sweat, rest.

A loud voice threatens. They let the water
trickle down their chins, necks, chests, legs

it waters the ground, wets the appetites
of the owners sitting in some far away place,
sipping ice cold tequila, chewing the worm
at the end of each bottle.

"Man Smoking"
Vincent Van Gogh, 1888

In 100 years he will be my late grandfather.
Plastic for a stomach. Doctors excuses.

Today his blue hat is the sky, it covers
his body like a bubble, protecting his skin
from the sun, the eyes of strangers.

His coat is nicotine, his corncob
pipe holds the break at the end of a day
working in the clouds, making rainbows,
to color the tobacco in the wide fields at his feet.

His friends move and pick, move and pick, chewing
the leaves like cows.

At night, smoke is the air; it seasons their food,
dyes their clothes, breathes for them.

DAYDREAM
Vincent Van Gogh,
Mlle. Gachet in Her Garden at Auvers-sur-Oise, 1890

Forced into marriage at a young age,
she became a dream her daughters
told, a casual story over tea.

Described in short dunks, her childhood
a tiny bite moved to the corner of a mouth
too young to know what it was in for

her teenaged years, time to ask for refills
from servants lining walls like plants.

Womanhood was the last sip of tea, moments
when she tired of hiding in the drapes to listen,
would slip quietly out into what was supposed
to be hers—but what was always her husband's garden,
to add poison to each of his carefully
nurtured, prized flowers

IRISES
Vincent Van Gogh, *Vase with Irises*, 1890

The vase is a brown hand
picking sky from sky.
It rearranges the best
part of eyes among
stems green as
pine needles..
Stick a
needle in
each eye
and the
sky falls
somewhere
far away,
the sun stops
covers the
moon like a
large room
and every iris
in the world—
goes blind.

OTHER BOOKS BY BOTTOM DOG PRESS

An Unmistakable Shade of Red & The Obama Chronicles
by Mary E. Weems
978-1-933964-18-8   80 pgs, $15

Ascent from Cleveland: Wild Heart Steel Phoenix
by Russell Salamon
978-1933964-19-5   80 pgs. $14

Cleveland Poetry Scenes: A Panorama and Anthology
eds. Nina Gibans, Mary Weems, Larry Smith
978-1933964-17-1 304 pgs. $20

d.a.levy & the mimeograph revolution
eds. Ingrid Swanberg & Larry Smith
1-933964-07-3 276 pgs. & dvd $25

Our Way of Life: Poems
by Ray McNiece
978-1-933964-14-0 128 pgs. $14

The Search for the Reason Why: New and Selected Poems
by Tom Kryss
0-933087-96-9 192 pgs. $14

Hunger Artist: Childhood in the Suburbs
by Joanne Jacobson
978-1-933964-11-9 132 pgs. $16

America Zen: A Gathering of Poets
eds. Ray McNiece and Larry Smith
0-933087-91-8 224 pgs. $15

Evensong: Contemporary American Poets on Spirituality
eds. Gerry LaFemina & Chad Prevost
ISBN 1-933964-01-4 276 pgs. $18

Order Online at:
http://members.aol.com/Lsmithdog/bottomdog

CPSIA information can be obtained at www.ICGtesting.com
Printed in the USA
269079BV00002B/9/P